# EXTREME SPORTS

## SPORTS

### AND THEIR GREATEST COMPETITORS

# in side sports

# EXTREME SPORTS

AND THEIR GREATEST COMPETITORS

EDITED BY HOPE LOURIE KILLCOYNE

## Britannica

Educational Publishing

IN ASSOCIATION WITH

## ROSEN

EDUCATIONAL SERVICES

Published in 2015 by Britannica Educational Publishing (a trademark of Encyclopædia Britannica, Inc.) in association with The Rosen Publishing Group, Inc.
29 East 21st Street, New York, NY 10010

Distributed exclusively by Rosen Publishing.
To see additional Britannica Educational Publishing titles, go to rosenpublishing.com.

First Edition

**Britannica Educational Publishing**
J. E. Luebering: Director, Core Reference Group
Anthony L. Green: Editor, Compton's by Britannica

**Rosen Publishing**
Hope Lourie Killcoyne: Executive Editor
Additional content supplied by Dan Harmon
Nelson Sá: Art Director
Nicole Russo: Designer
Cindy Reiman: Photography Manager

**Library of Congress Cataloging-in-Publication Data**

Extreme sports and their greatest competitors/edited by Hope Lourie Killcoyne.—First Edition.
    pages cm.—(Inside Sports)
"Distributed exclusively by Rosen Publishing"—T.p. verso.
Includes bibliographical references and index.
Audience: Grades: 5–12.
ISBN 978-1-62275-596-7 (Library bound)
1. Extreme sports—History—Juvenile literature. 2. Athletes—Rating of.
GV749.7.E987 2015
796.04'6—dc23

# CONTENTS

# INTRODUCTION

What makes a sport "extreme"? It's a tricky question. Most sports, even those that call for simple running and swimming skills, entail certain risks. At the same time, not all dangerous forms of recreation qualify as sports. Bungee jumping, for instance, requires lots of nerve but no particular skill.

Most extreme sports involve practiced skills and competitions with comparatively high risks of injury. In many of these "alternative" sports, as they're sometimes called, high speed accounts for the risks. Examples include freestyle skiing, street luge, skateboarding, snowboarding, in-line roller skating, BMX, and motocross. Racing and acrobatic competitions for motorcycles and snowmobiles usually are classified as extreme. The definition can also include such pursuits as rock climbing and skydiving.

Many of today's extreme sports were on the fringe of serious athletic competition

*Christi Brown, seen here smiling at about 10,000 feet (3,000 m) above Gardiner, N.Y., on July 26, 2014, has been skydiving since 2012. Her arms are positioned in a way she says helps stabilize her "sitfly." After leaving the aircraft, she free-falls for about sixty seconds, then parachutes.*

until the 1990s. Surfers, skateboarders, parachutists, and rock climbers were admired and respected for their skills. However, their activities were considered recreation, not sport.

To many people, the term "extreme sports" is associated with the X Games. This festival of high-risk, alternative competitions was introduced in 1995 by the cable network ESPN. Televised X Games

have become enormously popular. Some of the sports featured in the early X Games have been added to the Summer and Winter Olympic Games.

But neither the X Games nor the Olympics encompass all of the sports that are considered extreme. Most everyone would agree that skydiving from a height of 24 miles (39 kilometers) is also extreme. So is spending a week exploring a pitch-black cave 5,000 feet (1,500 meters) beneath the surface of the earth.

The definition of extreme sports is changing and expanding year by year. Adventurous athletes constantly push the envelope. They look for riskier challenges to conquer and more clever ways to conquer them. Once they conquer them—and their rivals copy and then exceed what the origi-nators have done—those feats become less extraordinary. In time, what once was "push-ing the envelope" produces only yawns. Waterskiing, for example, was viewed as a daredevil phenomenon when it was invented in 1922. Today, the greatest hazard posed by waterskiing may be the fact that so many people are doing it, congesting lakes.

Along with profiles of notable competi-tors, this book breaks down extreme sports according to where they take place: from the sky and cliffs to snowy slopes; on streets, ramps, racetracks, and in arenas; and in caves, cragged canyons, and the deep blue sea.

Many of the extreme sports described here share a unique subculture that separates them from traditional team sports. It is a youth-oriented culture that has embraced new music and fashion and emphasizes individual creativity. Energetic young people are drawn to these sports because they offer individual freedom. At their own pace, aspiring athletes can learn, practice, progress, and ultimately excel. They can practice and perform alone or, when they want, with friends. Discipline and training are demanded, but they are self-imposed and self-paced.

However, readers who are interested in taking up these sports must not underestimate the danger. Loss of balance on a skateboard or skis can result in a life-changing injury for a novice. Failure to heed the weather can leave a caver or canyon explorer trapped, at the mercy of swiftly flooding waters. Read on, and learn more about the excitement—and the perils—of extreme sports.

# CHAPTER 1

## SNOWY SLOPES, CLIFFS, AND THE SKY ABOVE

Some risk takers love the challenge of clawing upward at a snail's pace. Others find their thrills plunging downward at incredible speeds. Hugging a rock face, skiing or snowboarding down a mountain slope, and hurtling from heights are all means of exhilaration. Many of these sports can be enjoyed by beginners. They also can be taken to extremes.

### SNOWBOARDING

Snowboarders sometimes call it "riding the mountains." Snowboarding combines techniques of skiing, skateboarding, and surfing.

*Chinese snowboarder Shuang Li started snowboarding competitively in 2008 at age 16. Here she is in the Women's Half-Pipe Qualification at the 2014 Winter Olympics in Sochi, Russia.* Iurii Osadchi/Shutterstock.com

10

Experimenters during the 1960s came up with the idea of surfing on snow. The crude boards they originally used have been perfected. Basically, a snowboard is like an extra-large skateboard without wheels. Bindings secure the rider's boots to the board, and an ankle leash keeps the board attached when the rider falls. On average, a snowboard is about 5 feet (150 centimeters) long and 10 inches (25 cm) wide. Some boards are narrower in the middle, which makes them easier to turn. Unlike snow skiers, snowboarders use no poles.

Dedicated snowboarders train for different styles of competition, including Alpine, freestyle, and boardercross (also called snowboard cross). Each style requires different skills and calls for specialized boards and boots.

Alpine snowboarding involves little jumping. Rather, athletes maneuver around gates in a succession of turns, competing against the clock. Slalom and giant slalom events have tight turns and require exceptional technical expertise. The supergiant slalom is on a longer course with looser turns. Taking the turns as fast as possible with their bodies leaning close to the snow is second nature to Alpine snowboarders.

Freestyle snowboarding involves jumps and tricks. Freestyle often takes place on a half-pipe, a semicircular ramp built from snow that resembles the bottom portion of a tube. Snowboarders ride back and forth on the half-pipe, performing tricks as they go airborne at each end. They are judged on their spins, somersaults, and other aerial maneuvers. Freestyle snowboarders also ride in parks, urban settings, and other locations. They use natural and manmade features that include ramps, rails, concrete fixtures, rocks, boxes, rooftops, and logs. Slopestyle is a form of freestyle in which competitors perform jumps and tricks while also racing down a course.

In boardercross contests, four to six riders at a time negotiate a downhill course that presents them with bumps, berms, jumps, and other obstructions. Accidental collisions among boardercross riders are not uncommon.

The Fédération Internationale de Ski (International Ski Federation) governs snowboarding competition. Giant slalom and half-pipe competitions were introduced as Winter Olympic sports in 1998. Snowboard cross events became an Olympic event in 2006, and both parallel slalom and slopestyle were added in 2014.

## *FREESTYLE SKIING*

Snow skiing can be particularly dangerous in certain circumstances. Adding acrobatics on a downhill run—freestyle skiing—takes it to an extreme. As with other extreme sports, freestyle skiing is growing in popularity. On-site spectators and television viewers are riveted by each performance. They marvel at the daring and graceful, seemingly impossible acrobatics and landings. They also anticipate the inevitable crashes.

The origins of freestyle date back to the early 1900s. Skiers experimented with somersaults and other tricks before 1914 and popularized them in competitions in the early 1920s. One of the first freestyle events was acro, also known as ballet, which was invented in the 1930s in Europe. Using acrobatic moves borrowed from figure skating and gymnastics, acro skiers performed jumps, spins, and flips set to music while skiing on a gently sloping hill. In the 1950s and '60s, "hot dog" skiers in the United States began practicing more daring stunts. In 1980–81 the Fédération Internationale de Ski designated freestyle skiing an official sport. It was introduced at the Winter Olympics in 1992.

For a number of years there were two major categories of freestyle in international competition: aerials and moguls. Aerials are somersaults, twists, and other tricks performed in the air. Upright aerials include jumps such as the spread eagle, with arms and legs momentarily flung out to the side, and the daffy, with one ski extended forward, the other backward. Inverted aerials include stunts in which the skier's feet are higher than the head, such as somersaults and flips. Inverted stunts may reach heights of 50 feet (15 m). In competition, the run is scored based on form and technique, takeoff and height achieved, and landing.

Mogul skiing requires competitors to navigate large bumps, called moguls, on the slope. The run is judged on speed, turn techniques, and two required upright jumps. In many of their breathtaking jumps, skiers can't see the landing points until the final second or two.

The popularity of aerial and mogul events encouraged the development of other freestyle forms. In ski cross, four competitors race together down a challenging course of jumps, banked turns, and other features. It became an Olympic event in 2010. Slopestyle and half-pipe contests were added to the

# SLOPESTYLE: TOO DANGEROUS FOR PRIME TIME?

Slopestyle skiing and snowboarding are two of the most exciting events to perform and watch. They're also two of the most controversial because of the injuries that have occurred at major events. In slopestyle, competitors speed down courses featuring rails and other unnatural objects as well as standard jumps. They perform a variety of stunts while airborne.

Slopestyle skiing and snowboarding are especially popular at the annual Winter X Games. They became Olympic events at the 2014 Games in Sochi, Russia. Crashes and injuries were common in Sochi—too common, in the opinion of experts. Some athletes blamed the Sochi slopestyle course, the largest to date. Snowboarding star Shaun White withdrew from competition, believing the injury risk there was excessive. Lars Engebretsen, an orthopedic surgeon and International Olympic Committee official, afterward said the slopestyle injury rate at Sochi was "too high to be a sport that we have in the Olympics."

Olympics in 2014. Called freeskiing, these styles employ skis with raised tips at both ends. This allows skiers to perform tricks while skiing either forward or backward.

# MOUNTAIN AND ROCK CLIMBING

Mountain climbers, or mountaineers, delight in one of the most grueling of all sports. Laborious hiking near the mountain base is the easy part. They ascend rugged, rocky slopes and icy inclines. They struggle inch by inch up sheer rock faces and overhangs.

Climbing calls for great strength, stamina, skill, and expertise with specialized gear. Months of vigorous training and conditioning precede major climbs. Usually two or more athletes climb together, which means teamwork is essential; the safety of all depends on each. Climbers carry basic survival gear for even short ascents. If the climb will take more than a day, they must pack along a tent, food, and sufficient water.

Rock slides are not uncommon, sometimes injuring climbers or leaving them in precarious positions. Along with the natural features of the mountain, weather can be an enemy. Climbers have been struck by lightning and caught in blinding snowstorms. Heavy snow accumulations can produce deadly avalanches.

Yet, the rewards are irresistible to dedicated climbers. Besides the satisfaction of achievement, they enjoy some of the most spectacular views in the world.

Many would-be mountain climbers are frustrated because the nearest peaks are hundreds or even thousands of miles away. They can satisfy their ambition by pursuing a related sport: rock climbing. Rock climbing originated as one aspect of mountain climbing. Climbers look for holes and cracks in a rock face, sometimes pulling themselves up by their fingers and toes. Besides physical strength, it requires excellent balance and mobility.

People have been climbing rock faces for centuries. Until the twentieth century, they used only their bare hands. Today, climbers use ropes, harnesses, anchors, carabiners, and other safety gear. If used properly, this equipment will catch the fall of a climber who slips.

There are different styles of rock climbing. In trad (traditional) climbing, climbers place protective devices such as pitons, nuts, and cams into rock openings to anchor safety ropes. Sport climbing is similar to trad climbing except that the anchors—mainly bolts—have already been attached to the wall. Aid climbing differs from these types in that climbers use equipment not only for protection but also to help them in their ascent. The most extreme form of climbing is free soloing, in which the climber uses no protection at all.

Adventurers can test their climbing skills not only on outdoor cliffs and pinnacles but at artificial climbing walls. Some walls are indoors, making the sport doable in any season or weather. In some competitions, participants race up a rock wall together; in others, they each climb a designated route, striving for the best time.

Ice climbing is a form of rock climbing with unique difficulties. Using handheld ice tools and spiked boots, climbers make their way up surfaces such as ice-covered rock slabs and frozen waterfalls.

A simpler, safer form of rock climbing is bouldering. Here, the climber takes on a large rock that is only 10 to 20 feet (3 to 6 m) high. No climbing tools are used; padding on the ground below softens a fall.

## SKYDIVING, PARACHUTING, AND OTHER AIRBORNE SPORTS

Historical sketches trace the concept of the parachute—an overhead canopy that permits a person to descend earthward slowly and safely from great heights—to more than 500 years ago. The word "parachute," translated from its French root, means "to protect from a fall."

The first person to use a modern parachute was André-Jacques Garnerin. In Paris in 1797, he attached an umbrella-shaped cloth canopy to a large basket using ropes. With this canopy connected to a hydrogen balloon, he rode in the basket to a height of about 3,200 feet (1,000 m) and cut his contraption loose. He landed safely, despite spinning alarmingly on the way down. Garnerin learned that by cutting a hole in the center of the parachute he could stabilize the airflow and gain better control while descending. His wife, Jeanne-Genevieve, was the first woman parachutist.

Parachuting improved greatly over the next two centuries. Military engineers perfected basic, reliable chutes for dropping troops—a few commandos, or thousands at a time—behind enemy lines. Adventurers, meanwhile, looked for ways to take parachuting to extremes.

Experienced skydivers usually jump from altitudes of 7,500 to 15,000 feet (2,300 to 4,600 m). They free-fall for about a minute, sometimes a little longer. Then, at approximately 2,500 feet (760 m), they open the parachute and waft down for a gentle landing.

The speed of the free fall depends on the type of jumpsuit the skydiver wears and the angle of the diver's body to the ground. A

# BASE JUMPING: SPORT OR STUNT?

BASE jumping is parachuting, but not from an airplane. Rather, BASE jumpers leap from atop fixed locations. The sport takes its name from the four types of objects from which the parachutists jump: Building, Antenna, Span (bridge), and Earth (cliff or mountain). Veteran BASE jumpers have made hundreds—some of them thousands—of jumps. Their ambition is to exercise their skills and daring in a variety of locations, each with its unique challenges and rewards. Some have traveled the world in their quests.

*A man BASE jumps into a valley in South Africa.* **Cavan Images/ Stone/Getty Images**

The dangers of BASE jumping are acute. The reason is the short time between jumping and landing. While skydivers have several minutes to free-fall, relishing the rising landscape below them and their eerie aerial freedom before they leisurely open their chutes, BASE jumpers have just seconds. In 2000, Tom Aiello, an experienced BASE jumper, almost died in a 486-foot (148 m) leap from a bridge in Idaho. It was a five-second fall, and he deployed his chute too late. He hit the river below at 80 miles (130 km) per hour. Aiello lived but spent three months in the hospital, completely unable to move for the first three weeks.

Now a BASE instructor, Aiello tells his students to "expect to get injured." Most long-time BASE jumpers, he says, sooner or later are hospitalized.

Not surprisingly, BASE jumping is illegal in many places.

loose-fitting suit and a spread-eagle, facedown falling posture slow the fall. The typical free-fall rate is about 120 miles (195 km) per hour. Skydivers in speed competitions, plunging headfirst, attain free-fall speeds of greater than 300 miles (480 km) per hour.

For safety, skydivers wear reserve parachutes to deploy in case the main chute fails to open. They also wear altimeters to show their descending height so they will know when they need to activate their chutes.

The words "skydiving" and "parachuting" often are used synonymously. Similar airborne sports have also become popular. Different types of parachutes and other gear have been developed for these aerial pursuits.

## Hang Gliding and Paragliding

These related sports enable a skilled pilot to fly great distances without powered propulsion. Unlike skydivers, who can control only the rate and direction of their fall, hang gliders and paragliders can maintain altitude and even rise by locating thermals in the atmosphere. The principle is much like soaring in a glider or hot-air balloon, but without an aircraft frame or balloon basket for the pilot. Rather, the pilot rides suspended beneath a type of wing. Some pilots are experts in both hang gliding and paragliding.

Scientists and visionaries dreamed of flying for centuries before the invention of the airplane. Among the pioneers was Otto Lilienthal. Experimenting with wings not unlike those of today's hang gliders, he achieved flights as long as 800 feet (240 m). Lilienthal died in 1896 after losing control

*Otto Lilienthal is shown here in one of his last flights, in August 1896, in Germany.* **Keystone-France/Gamma-Keystone/Getty Images**

of a glider and crashing from a height of 50 feet (15 m).

A hang glider is a light metal frame with synthetic cloth wings fixed atop it; the wings may be flexible or rigid. The pilot lies in a cocoon-like harness suspended below the wings, gripping a frame bar and controlling flight by shifting weight. Hang-gliding competitions typically involve flying cross-country to a landing site, passing waypoints. Stunt pilots perform tricks such as barrel rolls and loops.

A paraglider, unlike a hang glider, has no rigid frame. Rather, it consists of a harnessed pilot seat attached by lines to a flexible cloth wing. The wing resembles a parachute, but its design takes advantage of aerodynamics to allow prolonged flights. Takeoff and landing are on foot and usually occur on a hill or mountain. In flight, the pilot controls the wing using lines attached to the trailing edge of the paraglider. Competitions include cross-country routes with designated waypoints to cross.

Depending on the weather, terrain, and the person's skill, a hang-gliding or paragliding flight can last for several hours or longer and cover great distances and altitudes. Soaring above 10,000 feet (3,000 m) is not unusual. In South Africa in 2008 paraglider Nevil Hulett covered a record straight-line distance of 313 miles (503 km) and was in the air 7 hours and 39 minutes. In 2012, two hang-gliding pilots in Texas flew more than 470 miles (756 km) in about 11 hours; Dustin Martin set the distance record of 475 miles (764 km), slightly ahead of his companion, Jonny Durand.

Pilots can attain remarkable speeds. Paragliders can reach 35 miles (56 km) per hour. Hang gliders have exceeded 100 miles (160 km) per hour in competitions, though the average speed is much lower than that.

Although they will always be risky, hang gliding and paragliding have been made safer over the years. Altimeters, reserve parachutes, and other safety and control devices have become standard equipment.

## Wingsuit Flying

Wingsuiters resemble Superman darting through the air. The sensations they experience match those that viewers of action films can only imagine. As they leap from a precipice or airplane, the air catches and inflates their specially designed jumpsuits, allowing them to zoom forward very, very fast.

Paragliding and hang gliding more effectively duplicate birdlike soaring, but they require attached wings to gain lift. In a wingsuit, wings become part of the person's body. The suit, made of highly durable synthetic fabric, stretches weblike between the legs and under the arms.

*The thrill and beauty of human "flight" is displayed by this wingsuiter jumping off a mountain in Norway.* **Evgeniya Moroz/ Shutterstock.com**

Wingsuiters can't soar as paragliders and hang gliders do. Their bodies constantly descend, though not nearly as fast as those of skydivers. They deploy parachutes at the end of their flights for safe landings, though stunt divers have made water landings without chutes. Practically all wingsuiters have extensive skydiving experience.

The great thrill is the speed they can reach while flying almost horizontally, maneuvering closely around mountains and through tight spaces, sometimes performing aerial acro-batics. Wingsuiters often fly faster than 100 miles (160 km) per hour. They also can travel considerable distances. In 2012, Shinichi Ito flew 17.8 miles (28.6 km) in California before deploying his parachute.

## SPACE DIVING

What's the highest altitude from which a parachutist can jump and survive? That's the question space divers seek to answer.

For more than 50 years, the record-high jump was the August 1960 epic jump by Col. Joseph Kittinger, a U.S. Air Force pilot. Kittinger was involved in a project to deter-mine whether pilots could safely bail out of an airplane or spacecraft flying in the strato-sphere. After ascending with the aid of a helium balloon, he made two test jumps from an altitude of approximately 75,000 feet (23,000 m), or about 14 miles (23 km). For his third and final jump, he ascended to approxi-mately 102,800 feet (31,300 m)—some 19.5 miles (31.4 km)—before stepping out of the gondola. He free-fell for more than four-and-a-half minutes and opened his chute at 17,500 feet (5,300 m). During the fall, his body reached a speed of 614 miles (988 km) per hour.

*gh-altitude free fall of Air Force pilot Joseph Kittinger,
60. The clouds beneath him are 15 miles (24 km) away.
ed, he reports having said, "Lord, take care of me now."*
**Pictures/The LIFE Picture Collection/Getty Images**

Felix Baumgartner, an Austrian skydiver, broke Kittinger's record in October 2012. A helium balloon lifted him to an altitude of nearly 128,000 feet (39,000 m), or 24 miles (39 km). During his free fall, which lasted four minutes and 20 seconds, he reached a record speed of 844 miles (1,358 km) per hour, breaking the sound barrier. At one point he spun wildly out of control. Baumgartner was able to stabilize himself and safely open his parachute.

Record keepers point out that space divers are not jumping literally "from the edge of space," as news headlines have claimed. Space technically begins about 62 miles (100 km) above Earth's surface.

# CHAPTER 2

## STREETS, RAMPS, RACETRACKS, AND BEYOND

**W**heel sports of every imaginable sort captivate thousands of athletes and millions of fans. Bike and skate vehicles are popular in extreme sports circles—especially when used in vert (short for "vertical") competitions to perform aerial stunts. Other adventurers take to their feet in parkour, simulate military ground combat in extreme paintball, or ride zip-lines over scenic terrain.

### SKATEBOARDING

The rider stands balanced on a board with wheels, controlling the ride by constantly shifting the feet and body weight. With practice, skateboarders learn to perform increasingly difficult stunts. Some invent their own tricks and combinations.

Most skateboards are approximately 32 inches (81 cm) long and 9 inches (23 cm) wide. They are made of wood, plastic, aluminum, or fiberglass. The rear end, and on some boards also the front, is curled slightly upward. The rider uses this kicktail for turning and other maneuvers. A variation of the skateboard is the longboard, which can be as long as 60 inches (153 cm). Special skateboards fitted with sails use windpower to push them forward. Boards with blades instead of wheels are used on ice.

Crude skateboards—consisting of roller-skate wheels attached to a board—appeared a century ago. Manufactured skateboards became popular in the 1960s, offering "sidewalk surfing" as an alternative to ocean surfing. Modern boards with polyurethane wheels and kicktails are faster and more maneuverable.

Riders perform two main styles of sport skateboarding: vert and street style. Vert skating, performed in half-pipes, features aerial tricks at astonishing heights. In street-style skating, riders in urban settings perform stunts using rails, stairs, ledges, and other artificial structures. Basic maneuvers include the kickturn (lifting the front wheels and spinning around on the rear wheels) and the ollie (jumping with the feet and board together).

Skateboard competitions began in 1963. Large competitions governed by World Cup Skateboarding are held in many countries. The televised X Games, sponsored by the cable television network ESPN, have been a major factor in the growing popularity of skateboarding. They include men's and women's professional skateboarding events.

Perhaps the most dramatic professional event in skateboarding is the Big Air competition at the X Games. Riders speed down a long "mega ramp," launch into the air, land on a quarter-pipe, and finish with a high vertical ascent off the end with an upright landing. During the airborne phases, they perform rotations and other tricks.

*With a crowd of onlookers in his wake, a man skateboards down a hill in New York City's Central Park, 1965.* **Bill Eppridge/Time & Life Pictures/Getty Images**

# The X Games: An Extreme Sports Extravaganza

ESPN launched the X Games (initially called the Extreme Games) in the summer of 1995. Games have been held each summer in the United States since then. Annual winter games began in 1997. The X Games expanded to Asia in 1998 and were held in Europe from 2010 through 2013.

Professional athletes from around the world have competed for medals and cash prizes in dozens of extreme sports. Events vary each year. Summer X Games have included different categories of skateboarding, BMX, mountain biking, motocross, aggressive in-line roller skating, street luge, and more. Among the winter sports are snowboarding, skiing, snowmobiling, and ice climbing. The X Games draw thousands of fans in person and have been broadcast in more than 200 countries.

## In-Line Roller Skating

In-line skates are a type of roller skate consisting of boots with a single row of wheels along the bottom. This in-line wheel arrangement makes the skates faster and more maneuverable than traditional roller skates, which have two wheels in front and two in back. In the 1980s, an improved type of in-line skates, known by the brand name Rollerblades, was embraced by speed skaters, roller-hockey players, and recreational skaters.

Skilled skaters developed tricks and competitions much like those of skateboarding. This discipline is called aggressive in-line skating. In street style in-line skating, skaters in urban environments do stunts with rails, stairs, and other structures. Vert skating, similar to vert skateboarding, features aerobatics off half-pipes and ramps. Both aggressive in-line and vert skating have been included in the X Games.

## STREET LUGE

If racing down a paved incline on a roller board—while lying on your back and peeking over your legs at the road ahead—appeals to you, consider street luge. The sport began when experimenters tried lying prone on longboard-type skateboards. The luge boards that evolved from that have different designs but are, in effect, all skateboards themselves. They are as long as 8.5 feet (2.6 m). A padded

# SKATING *EXTREMELY* SLOWLY

Extreme sports, for the most part, are dangerously fast. John Kitchin, a retired doctor living in San Diego, Calif., takes in-line skating to the opposite extreme. Well-known along the waterfront boardwalk, he's seen every day—sometimes for hours on end—gracefully, slowly gliding among strollers, cyclists, and skateboarders. Leaning forward, arms outstretched, always smiling, he's a skater who's in it for the motion and the sense of freedom. Speed doesn't matter at all.

*Kitchin in action*—slow *action.* © Crissy Pascual/U-T San Diego/ ZUMA Wire

He's known locally as "Slomo."

Kitchin, born in 1943, gave up a high-paying career as a neurologist in 1998. Despite owning a mansion and expensive cars, he was tired of his materialistic lifestyle. He retired to a beachside studio apartment. He enjoys writing, art, and music, but his greatest enjoyment comes from in-line skating in slow motion. Despite a vision disorder (or perhaps, he believes, because of it), he has exceptional balance on skates.

Regulars on the boardwalk greet him with smiles and high-fives. Until 2013, when a documentary about him went viral on YouTube, most of them knew nothing of his past. Many thought he was homeless. Regardless, they all are impressed by the man who's found his extreme sports passion—at slow speed.

support at the rear props up the rider's head a little. Some recreational street luges have handlebars and allow the rider to sit upright. On some courses, street luges go as fast as 80 miles (130 km) per hour.

Two organizations oversee street luge competition. The International Gravity Sports Association (IGSA) determines annual world champions in street luge as well as classic luge and downhill skateboarding. The International Downhill Federation (IDF) sponsors events in the same sports and maintains competitor rankings in each.

## BMX AND MOUNTAIN BIKING

Bicycle motocross (BMX) requires exceptional strength, stamina, and mobility. The sport takes two forms: BMX racing and freestyle BMX. In BMX racing, competitors ride on dirt tracks that feature many jumps and turns. BMX racing is very popular in the United States, Europe, and Australia. It debuted as an Olympic sport in 2008. Freestyle BMX emphasizes acrobatics rather than racing. Freestyle riders perform such aerial tricks as backflips, spins, and combinations. Street riders take on rails, steps, curbs, and other objects. Some riders specialize in verts, using half-pipes to enable aerial stunts.

Another off-road pursuit, mountain biking, is more of an endurance sport, though some riders also engage in jumps and tricks. Mountain bikes are designed to take rough terrain, and mountain bikers relish the tests of strength and stamina. Mountain bike racing became an Olympic event at the 1996 Games.

The International Mountain Bicycling Association builds and maintains trails and promotes the sport. Union Cycliste Internationale, based in Switzerland, sponsors BMX, mountain bike, and other cycling disciplines.

## MOTOCROSS

Motocross is essentially the motorized version of BMX racing, though on a greater scale. The course, typically about a mile long (1.6 km), consists of open, mostly rough terrain. Challenges include mud, steep hills, and difficult turns. Indoor competitions called supercross are run inside large arenas on artificial dirt tracks. Though the courses are usually shorter than those in motocross, they feature longer and more frequent jumps.

In freestyle motocross, riders launch from hills or artificial ramps to get airborne. They perform aerial

*An extreme motocross jump is seen here in midflight at the 2014 Kia World Extreme Games in the Chinese city of Shanghai.* **AFP/ Getty Images**

stunts such as backflips, seat grabs (extending the legs backward while holding the seat), and surfers (standing on the seat in a surfing position while holding the handlebars).

Motocross bikes are lightweight and can go very fast. Although races last no more than 40 minutes, motocross is considered possibly the most physically demanding motorcycle sport.

International competition is supervised by the Fédération Internationale de Motocyclisme. World championship series are held annually in each of three classes, which are determined by engine size.

## EXTREME PAINTBALL

Millions of people have let off steam with paintball. Gradually, paintball has become a professional as well as recreational sport. A few top players are paid for endorsing products, although most have other careers.

Paintball is played in a variety of environments, including woods, fields, and building interiors. A game may involve only a few players or teams of hundreds. In XBall, an extreme variation of the sport, competing teams try to retrieve a flag posted in the center of the playing field.

The number of tournaments—professional or amateur—is on the rise. Hundreds of teams from around the world compete for the Paintball World Cup. It is sponsored by Paintball Sports Promotions (PSP), a professional league that holds events across the United States. Professional players have lobbied to have paintball introduced at the X Games.

## PARKOUR

In a nutshell, the objective of parkour is to get from one point to another, overcoming whatever obstacles are in the way. The French word *parcours* means "the course" or "the way through." A parkour course might call for running, crawling, leaping, climbing, vaulting, or swinging. Athletes often perform acrobatics along the way. The idea for parkour stemmed from the obstacle courses used in military training. No equipment is needed: simply lightweight, casual clothes and good running shoes.

A person who engages in parkour is called a *traceur* (if male) or *traceuse* (if female). Enthusiasts point out the sport's positive mental and physical values. The World Freerunning and Parkour Federation describes the sport as a "philosophy. . . . It's a

way of looking at any environment and believing in your heart that there is no obstacle in life that cannot be overcome."

## ZIP-LINING

Zip-lining is a way for practically anyone to get a taste of extreme pursuits without training, conditioning, or serious risks. A steel cable called a zip-line or zip-wire is stretched down a long slope or across a scenic valley. A pulley is attached to the cable, and a handle-bar, seat, or harness hangs below the pulley. The rider either holds onto the handlebar or uses the seat or harness to travel down the zip-line. A handbrake lets the rider control the speed of descent.

*Zip-lining in an Ecua rain forest.* Ammit Ja Shutterstock.com

Children's playground lines, called flying foxes, are just high enough for the body to clear the ground. At the extreme, cables at some professional courses are as high as 2,500 feet (760 m) above valley floors. A zip-line in Peru called the Eye of the Jaguar is about 1.3 miles (2.1 km) long. Professional zip-liners have descended at speeds of almost 100 miles (160 km) per hour.

# CHAPTER 3

## CAVES, CANYONS, AND THE DEEP BLUE SEA

While some adventurers go for alpine heights, others are drawn to the extreme depths of caves and canyons. Those destinations present rewards—and risks—of a different sort. And while some take to the air and defy the pull of gravity, others take to the water and defy the forces of surf and wind.

### CAVING

Caves have long fascinated both scientists (speleologists) and sport cavers, sometimes called spelunkers. Sport caving has become increasingly popular worldwide for its mystery, underground grandeur, and hardy challenges. Some cavers go to extremes to explore hard-to-access, hazardous caves and

*A British caver treks through a stream in the reno...*
*Berger cave in southeastern France. A destination for ...*
*wide, at about two-thirds of a mile (more than 1,000 ...*
*filled with spectacular formations.* **Barcroft Media/G...**

caverns. Extreme cavers include teens as well as seniors.

Serious cavers sometimes embark on expeditions lasting for weeks, descending thousands of feet into the earth. Major cave systems open up amazing worlds. They may encompass underground rivers, pools, waterfalls, exotic stalactite and stalagmite formations, grotesque rock passageways, natural stairways, and huge chambers. A cave in the Sierra de Juárez Mountains in Mexico is some 8,500 feet (2,600 m) deep—possibly the world's deepest cave.

Deep caving is strenuous work, burning as much energy as bike racing. The hazards are many. Cavers have been hurt and killed by falls, falling rocks, cave-ins, entrapment in tight spaces, flooding, and hypothermia. Getting lost in an unfamiliar cave is not uncommon. Even with good lighting, the sensation can be quite claustrophobic. Burkhard Bilger, writing in *The New Yorker*, described caving as "a game played in the dark on an invisible field."

Dedicated cavers are known particularly as caretakers of nature. The National Speleological Society promotes safe caving practices that respect and maintain the underground environment and entrances.

## CANYONING

Canyoning, or canyoneering, involves much more than hiking into a canyon on well-worn trails. Canyoners must be technically equipped and experienced. Much of a canyoning adventure is like mountain climbing in the opposite direction—rappelling down rocky cliffs, sometimes alongside or through waterfalls. A bit of it involves climbing, sometimes by chimneying up narrow vertical passages. Canyoners scramble over rocky terrain, squeeze through tight passages, and sometimes have to swim.

They also hone practical skills: problem solving and route finding. At a canyon site sprawled over tens of thousands of acres, it's easy to become lost.

Canyoners in full gear appear to be a cross between mountain climbers and whitewater rafters. Apparatus includes helmet, wetsuit, ropes, packs, attached tools, and special shoes.

Experienced canyoners know to never go alone. Some of the same dangers of caving are present in canyoning. Flash floods are a special menace, since most canyons feature streams, rivers, and waterfalls. In a matter of seconds, canyoners have found themselves trapped in close confines under a deluge with no way out until the torrent subsides—which could be too late.

A significant reward of canyoning as either a sport or excursion is the natural beauty encountered. Canyoners are surrounded by enchanting rock types and formations.

## SURFING

The origins of surfing lie centuries in the past. When European explorers landed in Hawaii and Polynesia in the 1700s, they saw men and women wielding boards in the surf with great skill. After Hawaii became an international tourist attraction in the early 1900s, surfing became a worldwide sport. It has been

*A surfer competing in the 2012 Shark Island Challenge Final, Sydney, Australia.* **Matt King/Getty Images**

especially popular in California and Australia, which are noted for big-wave beaches. But it is enjoyed worldwide, even on coasts where incoming waves are moderate and the riding is fairly easy.

Competitive surfers travel great distances in quest of the "perfect wave." The perfect wave for one expert surfer can spell death for another who's equally skilled. As with most extreme sports, extreme surfing is marred by tragedies.

Surfboards are long, narrow, and lightweight, made of polyurethane and fiberglass. Average dimensions are 6 to 6.5 feet (1.8 to 2 m) long, 18 inches (45 cm) wide, and 2 inches (5 cm) thick. They weigh 5 to 6 pounds (2.3 to 2.7 kilograms). Shaped edges, noses, and tails, together with fins on the bottom, allow riders to move dancelike around a wave. Longer, specially designed boards are used in very heavy surf.

Surfers paddle their boards out to the area where swells begin to form into incoming waves. When a wave begins to surge, the surfer turns and paddles toward shore in front of it. The momentum of the wave propels the surfboard along. The surfer sits or kneels, striving to maneuver the board onto the curl of the wave just ahead of its crest. Then standing, if possible, the surfer rides down the rising wall of water. The classic surfing maneuver is tubing, riding parallel to the incoming wave inside its looming, cascading curl.

Surfers move through the water as fast as 35 miles (56 km) per hour and are sometimes able to ride great distances along the beach. In 2014, Steve King of Great Britain broke his own world distance record by riding a wave for 12.8 miles (20.6 km) along a river in Indonesia.

Common surfing tricks include hanging 10 (standing with all 10 toes over the nose of the board), floating the board along the top of an incoming wave, and doing headstands on the board. Extreme surfers go beyond that. In aerial surfing, the surfer rushes toward a vertical, cresting wave, rises on it, and launches into the air. The objective is to perform one or more stunts with the board in the two or three seconds available. Expert extremists—if they find the right wave—can execute a backflip while aloft in a move called the rodeo clown flip.

International surfing championships began in Hawaii in 1953. Professional surfers and advocates for years have campaigned to have surfing and related sports

# RULE NUMBER ONE: PLAY IT SAFE

It might not be noticed by viewers mesmerized by death-defying extreme sports footage in telecasts and videos, but most of the athletes who perform them take extreme precautions. Extreme athletes understand the risks. They accept the reality that a small, unexpected misstep can change their lives for the worse. Mainly what the audience sees is the "wow," and the wow can be deceptive.

That allure presents a serious problem when young adventurers—"amateurs without referees, coaches or medical personnel," as Jane E. Brody wrote in *The New York Times*—try it themselves. Brody's March 2014 article was titled "With the Thrills Come Extreme Risks." She cited statistics indicating that extreme sports accounted for more than 4 million injuries from 2000 through 2011.

Millions of teenagers aspire to follow in the paths of male and

**A rider falling off his BMX bike.**
Sergey Lavrentev/iStock/Thinkstock

*(continued on the next page)*

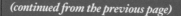

*(continued from the previous page)*

female athletes who take sports to the limits. "Unfortunately," Brody wrote, "many young people eager for an adrenaline rush are trying to copy their extreme sports idols, putting themselves at terrible risk. Filled with over-confidence, many participants lack the skills and training for these stunts. And often they fail to use safety equipment that could reduce the risk of serious injury."

Doctors, coaches, and other advisers emphasize the need for safety in all sports, but particularly in extreme sports. Safety measures include supervised training, mandatory safety equipment, on-site expert supervision, and professional medical aid.

incorporated into the Olympic Games. The International Surfing Association is the sport's governing body.

## WAKEBOARDING

Wakeboarding combines elements of surfing, waterskiing, snowboarding, and skateboarding. Standing on a foam board resembling a surfboard, the rider holds onto a rope that is pulled by a speedboat. Wakeboarders lean into the boat's roiling wake to cast themselves

*A wakeboard backflip.* Graham Legiehn/iStock/Thinks

into the air. They perform flips, rotations, and other stunts.

Wakeboarders are towed at moderate speeds, up to about 25 miles (40 km) per hour. This means they can be pulled by personal watercraft such as Jet Skis as well as by boat.

There are dozens of wakeboard moves. A flip is when a rider does a somersault in the air and lands with the wakeboard on the water. In a tantrum, the rider thrusts the heel of the board into the wake and launches into a backflip. There are many tantrum variations. Likewise, there are different ways to perform stunts approaching the wake with the toe end of the board. Grabbing the board in different ways in flight opens another category of maneuvers.

In competition, wakeboarders perform individual routines. They're judged on the difficulty of stunts, how well each one is executed, and the overall creativity of the sequence.

## WINDSURFING

Windsurfers are sailors as well as surfers. While surfers play against incoming beach waves, windsurfers use their boards as sailboats. They need skills and judgment to contend with wind and water conditions simultaneously.

Not all windsurfing is along a beach. It can be done in any body of water when a breeze is blowing, including rivers and lakes. Some competitions even take place indoors, with strong fans providing propulsion across vast pools. Windsurfing (also called sailboarding) is a Summer Olympic event.

There are many classes of windsurfing competition. Slalom, formula, and raceboard are racing events involving different types of courses, wind speeds and directions, and board designs. Wave riding incorporates stunts while riding and jumping surf waves. In big air jumps, athletes strive for the greatest height. Riders in freestyle are judged on the variety of tricks they successfully execute. Super X combines freestyle tricks and a slalom race.

Depending on conditions, speed is an added thrill of windsurfing. Surfers have reached speeds as high as 60 miles (97 km) per hour.

*A windsurfer hops over the water's foamy chop.* Ingram Publishing/ Thinkstock

# CHAPTER 4

## NOTABLE EXTREME SPORTS COMPETITORS

A thletes are constantly taking innovative sports to new extremes. Year-round, nonstop, they go higher, deeper, farther, faster, and crazier. Most extreme competitors are young adults or teens, but respected pioneers of past decades still amaze viewers with their daring, skills, creativity, and desire to surpass old accomplishments.

## SNOWBOARDING

### SHAUN WHITE

White—nicknamed the "Flying Tomato" because of his red hair—has won enough gold medals in snowboarding and skateboarding to practically start his own mint. In snowboarding they include two Olympic gold medals and 13

*Shaun White, 2012.* **Jean-Pierre Clatot/AFP/Getty Ima**

X Games championships. He's won gold in vert skateboarding twice at the X Games. He also has 10 ESPY (Excellence in Sports Performance Yearly) Awards and numerous other medals in slopestyle, half-pipe, and super-pipe snowboarding competition.

Overcoming an infantile heart defect that required two delicate operations, White began snowboarding at age six. He went pro at 13. Meanwhile, he was becoming a skateboarding whiz, tutored by legendary skateboarder Tony Hawk. White entered professional skateboarding competition at age 17.

White's performances have been dazzling. In one run at the 2006 Winter Olympics, he did two 1,080-degree spins (three complete body rotations) and one 900-degree spin. Although he placed a disappointing fourth in the half-pipe competition at the 2014 Winter Olympics, White remained one of the most popular Olympic competitors.

## FREESTYLE SKIING

### SARAH BURKE

Tragedy is an inevitable result of extreme sports. Numerous athletes have suffered debilitating injuries; some have died. Skiers and fans continue to mourn the death of Sarah Burke, considered the world's leading female freestyle skier.

The young Canadian won four X Games gold medals and helped gain Olympic status for half-pipe skiing competitors. She was the first woman to successfully perform a 1,080 in competition—completing three full body rotations in the air before landing.

Sarah Burke takes first place in the Fédération Internationale de Ski (International Ski Federation) Freestyle World Cup Women's Half-Pipe on March 20, 2011, La Plagne, France. Christophe Pallot/Agence Zoom/Getty Images

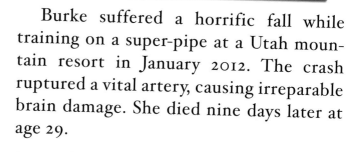

Burke suffered a horrific fall while training on a super-pipe at a Utah mountain resort in January 2012. The crash ruptured a vital artery, causing irreparable brain damage. She died nine days later at age 29.

## MOUNTAIN AND ROCK CLIMBING

### TORI ALLEN

As a child in the West African country of Benin, Tori Allen loved to climb trees, chasing her pet monkey Georgie. When she was 8, her family returned to the United States. She discovered that rock climbing was "what I was born to do," she writes on her blog, when she scaled a rock wall at a sporting-goods store. She set a national climbing record at age 11, became a professional rock climber at 12, and won an X Games gold medal at 14. When she was 13, she

*Tori Allen.* © **AP Images**

58

became the youngest female to summit El Capitan, a 3,000-foot (900 m) rock formation in Yosemite National Park. Her hand strength is extraordinary; she can hang from rocks by two fingers.

As a teenager, Allen also set a youth national record in pole vaulting. She attended Florida State University on a vaulting scholarship. After graduating with a degree in fashion design, Allen moved to Steamboat Springs, Colo., to take advantage of its many outdoor activities.

A motivational speaker, Allen has been outspoken against bullying. She explains that she was bullied in high school, mainly by other girl athletes.

## WINGSUITING AND BASE JUMPING

### JOBY OGWYN

Ogwyn is recognized for his accomplishments as a mountain climber, especially for his speed ascents. He also is renowned for BASE jumping and wingsuiting feats.

By the time he was 26, the Louisiana native had become the youngest person to

*visiting a New York
...dio on April 30, 2014.
...ty Images*

climb the Seven Summits—the highest mountains on each of the seven continents. Meanwhile, he set records as a BASE jumper. For example, he made three BASE jumps in one day from the treacherous north face of the Eiger peak in the Swiss Alps.

In May 2014, Ogwyn hoped to pull off one of the most amazing stunts in the history of extreme sports: a wingsuit jump from the top of Mount Everest. He already had made wingsuit flights around the different faces of the Matterhorn, a legendary challenge for climbers in the Alps. But during the trek up Everest, an avalanche killed 16 Sherpa guides. Rather than diving from the summit of the world's highest peak, Ogwyn—visibly shaken in news interviews—found himself joining rescue and recovery efforts.

## SKYDIVING

### DON KELLNER

With more than 41,000 jumps to his credit, Don Kellner holds the record for the most parachute descents. As his website proudly points out, "Each skydive that Don Kellner makes is a new world record."

Kellner is a U.S. Air Force veteran but, ironically, never made a parachute jump until he left the service. He began jumping in 1961 and has instructed countless skydiving students since then.

Kellner often jumps with his wife, Darlene. They were married in mid-air. Between them, they've made almost 60,000 jumps.

## SKATEBOARDING

### TONY HAWK

When Tony Hawk was 9 years old, his older brother gave him a worn-out skateboard to play with. By age 12 he was winning amateur

*on a vert ramp during a skating event for charity
, Calif., June 1, 2013.* Joe Scarnici/Getty Images

competitions in California, at 14 he turned pro, and by 16 he was considered the best skateboard competitor in the world. He competed in 103 professional events by age 25, winning 73. His victories included nine gold medals in the X Games. Hawk invented dozens of moves, mostly in vert skating. Among other milestones, he was the first skateboarder to successfully land a 900-degree aerial rotation (two-and-a-half body turns).

Hawk retired from professional skateboarding in 1999 at age 31, but his impact continues to be felt. He is one of the best-known extreme-sports athletes worldwide. The video-game series he endorses became one of the most popular ever among young gamers.

The Tony Hawk Foundation has funded more than 500 skateboard parks across the country, mainly in low-income neighborhoods. Hawk's autobiography, *Hawk: Occupation: Skateboarder*, became a bestseller.

# BMX

## MAT HOFFMAN

Many consider Mat Hoffman the best vert ramp competitor in BMX history. Since entering competition in 1985 at age 13, he's cleared 26.5 feet (8 m) above a quarter-pipe. He was the first rider to successfully complete a 180-degree spin in a backflip. He's the only rider to execute a hands-free 900-degree rotation in competition. And he's invented more than 100 BMX tricks.

Hoffman has combined BMX with other extreme sports—most notably, BASE jumping.

*...an takes to the sky at a skate park benefit event in* **Amanda Edwards/Getty Images**

He once biked off a 3,500-foot (1,070 m) cliff in Norway, landing safely with a parachute.

In addition to competing, Hoffman has contributed greatly to the promotion of the sport. The Hoffman Sports Association organizes freestyle BMX competitions around the world.

## EXTREME PAINTBALL

### ALEX LUNDQVIST

Born in Sweden, Alex Lundqvist formed a paintball team with his brother Max. They eventually were recruited by a professional team, Stockholm Joy Division. Moving to the United States, Lundqvist became a professional model—but he did not give up his love of paintball. He played for several pro teams, including the Russian Legion/Boston Red Legion of the Paintball Sports Promotions (PSP) National X-Ball League (NXL) and the Jersey Authority of the National Professional Paintball League (NPPL).

## SURFING

### KELLY SLATER

Dubbed "the Michael Jordan of professional surfing," Kelly Slater has won 11 Association of Surfing Professionals world championships. Born in 1972, he has the distinction of being the youngest *and* oldest surfer to win the title. He won five years in a row in the mid-1990s.

Slater was born in Cocoa Beach, Fla. He believes learning to surf in Florida's relatively tame waters gave him a valuable foundation for developing his skills. Even in his preteens, he began to demonstrate his prowess on the waves. He turned pro at 18 and won his first world championship at 20.

## WAKEBOARDING

### DALLAS FRIDAY

Before she was 10, Dallas Friday was already an accomplished gymnast. Burned out and losing interest in the sport, she was persuaded by her brother Robin, a wakeboarder, to take to the water. "I was hooked from that day forward and never looked back to gymnastics," she explains on her website. "I found a sport I loved and was destined to do."

By 13, Friday had become a formidable wakeboarding competitor. In 2001, at age 15, she won the Wakeboard World Cup. In 2004 Friday became the first wakeboarder to earn the ESPY (Excellence in Sports Performance Yearly) Award for Best Female Action Sports Athlete.

# WINDSURFING

## ROBBY NAISH

Son of noted surfer Rick Naish, Robby Naish bought his first windsurfing board and rig at age 12. The next year, 1976, he won his first windsurfing world championship. He was a dominant competitor into the 1990s, when he also began competing in kitesurfing. He won world kitesurfing titles in 1998 and 1999.

*Robby Naish.*
**Dean Treml/Getty Images**

Naish is legendary among windsurfers for his incredible maneuvers such as the forward loop (aerial somersault) and table top (a complex aerial rotation). He has written two books, appeared in films, and has been the subject of countless articles and videos. He markets a line of sailboards and other equipment. The business was started by his father, who designed windsurfing boards in the family garage. His personal philosophy, posted on his Facebook profile, is: "Life's what you make it . . . and every day on the water is a good day!"

# CONCLUSION

Safety has been a mounting concern in extreme sports, and professional athletes heed the warnings. It's worth noting that almost all extreme sports competitions, including zip-lining, require helmets at the very least. Improved safety equipment steadily is being developed. Governing organizations stipulate strict rules and require that equipment and competition facilities be inspected. Athletes discipline themselves to undergo rigorous practice and conditioning.

No degree of precautions, however, will eliminate injuries and fatalities entirely. By their nature, extreme sports involve higher risks than mainline sports. A study published in the *British Journal of Sports Medicine* indicated that one out of sixty BASE jumpers died in the year that they reviewed the sport. Some instructors frankly warn their students that if they make hundreds of jumps, they should expect to spend significant time in hospitals.

Those odds are severe enough to deter most athletes and adventurers. But extreme athletes take a different view. To them, danger is part of the appeal.

**aerodynamics** The qualities of an object that affect how easily it is able to move through the air.

**alpine** Referring to lofty mountains.

**altimeter** A device that measures the altitude of a plane or person in the sky.

**berm** A narrow ledge at the top or bottom of a slope.

**cam** Also called a spring-loaded camming device (SLCD), this metallic tool protects rock and mountain climbers by providing anchors for the climbing rope in rock crevices.

**carabiner** A spring-locked metal loop used to secure climbing ropes.

**chimneying** A climbing technique used in tight vertical shafts by canyoners, exerting opposite pressure against the walls with arms, feet, head, and back.

**claustrophobic** Intimidated by tight, enclosed spaces with no clear outlet for escape.

**commando** An elite fighter in a military special operations unit.

**free fall** The fast-descending part of a skydive before the parachute is deployed.

**gondola** An enclosed passenger compartment suspended beneath a hot-air or helium balloon.

**hypothermia** A dangerous drop in body temperature resulting from exposure to cold.

**inverted** Moving upside-down.

**materialistic** Preoccupied with money and possessions.

**mogul** A bump on a ski slope.

**nut** Also known as a stopper, this aluminum climbing tool is designed to slide into a wedge or crack in a rock to assist mountain and rock climbers.

**pipe** A structure used to facilitate aerial launches in various extreme sports. The most common, the half-pipe, resembles a pipe split horizontally; competitors speed down one wall and up the opposite, performing stunts when they become airborne. A super-pipe has higher walls. A quarter-pipe has just one wall.

**piton** A metal spike driven by climbers into rockface cracks to provide an anchor for support ropes.

**prone** Lying flat.

**propulsion** The force that moves an object or person forward.

**rappel** To descend by rope from a mountain height or rock face.

**roiling** Turbulent.

**slalom** A timed race down a zigzag course.

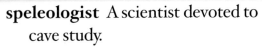

**speleologist** A scientist devoted to cave study.

**stalactite, stalagmite** Rock formations common in caves; stalactites point down from the cave roof while stalagmites point up from the floor.

**stratosphere** A layer of Earth's atmosphere between about 6 and 30 miles (10 and 50 km) above the surface.

**thermal** A column of rising air.

Adventure Drop, Inc.
334 Santana Row, Suite #330
San Jose, CA 95128
E-mail: staff@adventuredrop.com
Website: http://www.adventuredrop.com
With a focus on outdoor activities such
as bouldering, mountain biking, skydiving, windsurfing, and more, this
California-based organization provides
information about adventure-themed
activities and events in dozens of
places throughout the United States.
Adventurers are encouraged to share
their experiences with the Adventure
Drop community.

American Parkour Academy
219 M Street NW
Washington, D.C. 20001
(202) 642-1275
Website: http://americanparkour.com/
academy/washington-dc
The American Parkour Academy wel-
comes both absolute beginners and
experienced practitioners of all ages.
Its motto, "We believe in the power of
parkour to improve people's lives," is a
message that pervades its academy, community, and events.

Canadian Freestyle Ski Association
808 Pacific Street
Vancouver, BC V6Z 1C2
Canada
(604) 714-2233
Website: http://freestyleski.com
The association is the governing body for
     freestyle skiing in Canada.

Fédération Aéronautique Internationale
     (World Air Sports Federation)
Avenue de Rhodanie 54
1007 Lausanne
Switzerland
Website: http://www.fai.org
This international organization supports
     aeronautical and astronautical activi-
     ties, verifies records, and coordinates
     competitions.

Fédération International de Ski (FIS)
Marc Hodler House
Blochstrasse 2
CH-3653 Oberhofen / Thunersee
Switzerland
Website: http://www.fis-ski.com
The FIS, in cooperation with the International
     Olympic Committee, is the overall govern-
     ing entity for skiing.

International Surfing Association (ISA)
5580 La Jolla Boulevard, #145
La Jolla, CA 92037
(858) 551-8580
Website: http://www.isasurf.org
The ISA is recognized by the International
   Olympic Committee as the world governing authority for surfing, stand-up paddle
   surfing and racing, and all other wave-
   riding activities.

National Speleological Society (NSS)
6001 Pulaski Pike
Huntsville, AL 35810-1122
(256) 852-1300
Website: http://caves.org
The NSS works to further the exploration,
   study, and protection of caves and their
   environments and to foster fellowship
   among cavers.

United States Hang Gliding & Paragliding
   Association, Inc.
1685 West Uintah Street
Colorado Springs, CO 80904
(800) 616-6888, (719) 632-8300
Website: http://www.ushpa.aero
This organization promotes safe hang glid-
   ing and paragliding by fostering a sense of

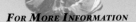

community among participants, helping develop and preserve flying sites, communicating a positive awareness of the sports to the public, and interacting with government agencies.

Worldwide Zip Line (WZL)
19123 Treend Road
Post Falls, ID 83854
Website: http://www.worldwidezipline.com
WZL educates people about the basic guidelines of zip-lining, showcases zip line–centric tours, and provides information about expert zip-line companies around the world.

## WEBSITES

Because of the changing nature of Internet links, Rosen Publishing has developed an online list of websites related to the subject of this book. This site is updated regularly. Please use this link to access this list:

http://www.rosenlinks.com/SPOR/Extr

Badillo, Steve. *Skateboarding: Legendary Tricks 2*. San Diego, CA: Tracks Publishing, 2010.

Benjamin, Daniel. *Extreme Rock Climbing* (Sports on the Edge!). New York, NY: Cavendish Square Publishing, 2014.

Brody, Jane E. "With the Thrills Come Extreme Risks." *New York Times*, March 31, 2014. Retrieved May 2014 (http://well.blogs.nytimes.com/2014/03/31/with-the-thrills-come-extreme-risks/?_php=true&_type=blogs&_php=true&_type=blogs&_r=1&).

Izenberg, Joshua. "Slomo." *New York Times*, March 31, 2014. Retrieved May 2014 (http://www.nytimes.com/2014/04/01/opinion/slomo.html?_r=2).

Jones, Cheryl. *A Guide to Responsible Caving*. Huntsville, AL: National Speleological Society, 2009.

Keh, Andrew. "Sarah Burke, Freestyle Skier, Dies from Injuries in Training." *New York Times*, January 19, 2012. Retrieved May 2014 (http://www.nytimes.com/2012/01/20/sports/skiing/sarah-burke-canadian-free-style-skier-dies-from-injuries.html?_r=0).

Mara, Wil. *Extreme BMX* (Sports on the Edge!). New York, NY: Cavendish Square Publishing, 2012.

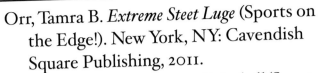

Orr, Tamra B. *Extreme Steet Luge* (Sports on the Edge!). New York, NY: Cavendish Square Publishing, 2011.

Otfinoski, Steven. *Extreme Paintball* (Sports on the Edge!). New York, NY: Cavendish Square Publishing, 2014.

Otfinoski, Steven. *Extreme Surfing* (Sports on the Edge!). New York, NY: Cavendish Square Publishing, 2011.

Romero, Jordan. *No Summit Out of Sight: The True Story of the Youngest Person to Climb the Seven Summits*. New York, NY: Simon & Schuster BFYR, 2014.

Woods, Mark, and Ruth Owen. *Xtreme!: Extreme Sports Facts and Stats*. New York, NY: Gareth Stevens Publishing, 2011.

# INDEX